PUBLISHED BY STUDIO PUBLICATIONS (IPSWICH) LIMITED
32 PRINCES STREET, IPSWICH, SUFFOLK, ENGLAND

Supercool is one of the Munch Bunch.

He is a very cool cucumber, who lives in a very cool flower-pot.

Supercool always wears his very cool hat and his very cool sneakers.

One day, Supercool was reading all about a new sport called skateboarding.

It looked great fun.

So he decided to make himself a skateboard.

He collected some old pieces of wood from the garden, and nailed them together.

Just like the pictures in his book.

All he needed now were some wheels.

"I know just the place," he thought to himself.

So he took the wheels off his bed.

Supercool's skateboard was ready for its first run.

He decided to try it out on the steepest hill he could find.

He passed Button and Tiny, the mushrooms, on his way up the hill.

"What's that thing under your arm?" asked Tiny.

"It's a skateboard," replied Supercool.

The mushrooms looked puzzled at Supercool's reply.

Supercool reached the top of the hill.

He didn't know that he should wear a helmet and some knee-pads.

He looked down the hill and saw some of the Munch Bunch playing.

There was Lizzie Leek and Tom Tomato, Sally Strawberry and Olly Onion, and Billy Blackberry and Scruff Gooseberry.

Supercool got on his skateboard and started to go down the hill.

"Wheeeee!" he cried. "This is great!"

The board ran faster and faster and faster. So fast that Supercool could not control it any more.

He could see Lizzie Leek and Tom Tomato getting closer and closer.

"Look out!" he cried.

Too late.

Supercool knocked them both over.

And Lizzie Leek's knitting got caught on the front of the skateboard.

Sally Strawberry was next.

CRASH!

Her brushes and paints flew into the air.

"Sorry!" yelled Supercool. "No brakes!"

And he raced on, totally out of control.

Faster and faster and faster he went.

Scruff Gooseberry saw him coming and jumped out of the way.

But poor Billy Blackberry didn't move quickly enough.

CRASH!

He ended up with the wool from Lizzie Leek's knitting tied round his legs.

Still Supercool raced on.

Then, DISASTER!

Supercool crashed into Olly Onion, who had been cycling up the hill.

Poor Olly Onion burst into tears.

Supercool's skateboard had not been built for such rough treatment.

CRACK!

It broke in half.

Supercool's feet left the skateboard, and he found himself flying through the air.

Right into a bush.

Head first.

With only his feet left sticking out.

The Munch Bunch pulled him out of the bush.

They were very angry.

Lizzie Leek's knitting was ruined.

Sally Strawberry's paint-brushes had fallen in the mud.

Billy Blackberry was covered in bruises, and Olly Onion was still crying.

Supercool was very upset.

He hadn't read the part in his book which showed him how to steer and stop a skateboard.

And now his skateboard had broken into pieces.

But Lizzie Leek gave him a parcel. "Here is a present for your birthday tomorrow," she said.

"Super!" cried Supercool.

"A brand-new skateboard!

"A helmet!

"Gloves!

"And some elbow- and knee-pads. Now I will be able to skate safely."

A.M.

The Munch Bunch laughed.

"Let's hope we will be safe, too," said Lizzie Leek.

Acknowledgement: This story of Supercool was adapted by Giles Reed from an original idea by Jim Raff.